J $9.95
527   Pollard, Michael
Po   Finding the way

DATE DUE

JY 15 93			
MAY 31 '94			
JUL 1 1 '95			
SEP 2 8 95			
NOV 2 9 95			
DEC 18 99			
SE 06 '00			
DE 08 '00			
MR 07 '01			
JY 31 '02			

DEMCO

MOVING AROUND THE WORLD
FINDING THE WAY

MICHAEL POLLARD

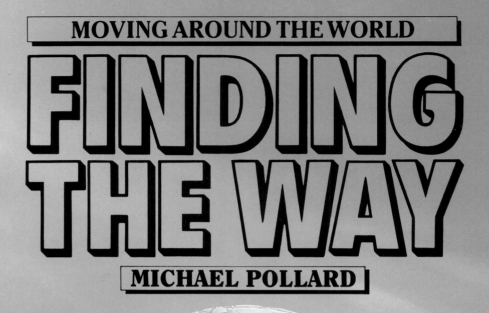

Editorial planning
Jollands Editions

SCHOOLHOUSE PRESS, *Inc.*

Copyright © 1986 by Schoolhouse Press, Inc.
4700 Rockside Road,
Independence, Ohio 44131
ISBN 0-8086-1043-0 (hardback)
ISBN 0-8086-1031-7 (paperback)

Original copyright, © Macmillan Education Limited 1986
© BLA Publishing Limited 1986

Designed and produced by BLA Publishing Limited,
Swan Court, East Grinstead, Sussex, England.
Also in LONDON · HONG KONG · TAIPEI · SINGAPORE · NEW YORK

A Ling Kee Company

Illustrations by Kevin Diaper, Sebastian Quigley/Linden
Artists, George Fryer/Linden Artists, Colin Newman/Linden
Artists, Alison Lawrenson, David Oakley and BLA Publishing
Limited
Color origination by Planway Limited
Printed in Italy by G. Canale & C. S.p.A. — Torino

85/86/87/88   6 5 4 3 2 1

Acknowledgements
**The Publishers wish to thank Cable and
Wireless plc for their invaluable assistance in the
preparation of this book.**

Photographic credits
t = top b = bottom l = left r = right

cover: ZEFA

4 ZEFA; 5*t* Stephen Krasemann/NHPA; 5*b*, 9*t*, 10*b* ZEFA; 16,
17*t*, 17*b* National Maritime Museum; 18 ZEFA; 21 National
Maritime Museum; 23*t*, 23*b* ZEFA; 33*b* NASA; 34 Andy
Williams/National Trust; 35*t* Peter Johnson/NHPA; 36*t*
G. Anderson/NHPA; 41*t*, 41*b*, 42*b* ZEFA; 43 Cable and
Wireless plc

Note to the reader
In this book there are some words in the text which are printed in **bold** type. This shows that the
word is listed in the glossary on page 46. The glossary gives a brief explanation of words which may
be new to you.

Contents

Introduction

When the first sailors set out to explore the world, they sailed along the coast. They felt safe because they were never far from land. Later, when they sailed off across the ocean, these first sailors soon lost sight of the land. They might sail for days or even weeks only seeing the sea and the sky. These first explorers had nothing to help them find their way.

▼ The line where the sky meets the sea is called the horizon. We cannot see beyond the horizon because the earth's surface is curved.

Finding the Way on Land

It is not only at sea that it is hard for people to find their way. On land, it may be just as difficult. In a desert, there may be nothing to see but sand. It is just as easy to get lost in a forest or in the icy lands of the Arctic.

The Movement of Animals

Some animals find their way over great distances without any help at all. They use their **instinct**, which is a natural way of doing things that all animals have. When birds fly to warmer countries in the winter months, this is called **migration**. Caribou, or reindeer, also migrate southwards from the Arctic in search of food. Even some butterflies fly hundreds of miles to lay their eggs.

▲ As winter approaches, herds of caribou move south to find food.

▼ In the desert, trucks have to keep to the marked tracks so that they do not lose their way.

Navigation

People do not have the same instinct as animals. Over thousands of years we have learned how to **navigate**, or find our way, with maps and **instruments**. Three things are necessary to navigate well. First, you must know where you are. Then, you must know the place or **position** you want to reach. You must also know the **direction** to take in order to get there.

This book tells the story of how people learned to navigate. We are going to start like the first explorers. These sailors had nothing to help them. They had, however, seen that the sun rose on one side of the sky every morning. It moved across the earth and set on the other side in the evening. Could they use the sun to point them in the right direction?

Using the Sun

The earth turns around completely once every 24 hours. As it **rotates**, light from the sun moves across the **surface** of the earth. Seen from the earth, the position of the sun in the sky changes continuously between sunrise and sunset. The sun always rises in the east and sets in the west. These are the two directions which are the same wherever you may be. Therefore, we can use the position of the sun to help us find our way.

Between sunrise and sunset the sun reaches its highest point in the sky at noon. At some places on the earth, the sun is directly overhead at noon. These places are all on the **Equator**. The Equator is an imaginary line around the middle of the earth. The part of the earth north of this line is called the Northern **Hemisphere**. The part to the south is the Southern Hemisphere.

Shipwrecked!

Imagine that you and some of your friends have been shipwrecked. Your sailboat has been swept ashore on a desert island. One of your friends thinks that there is land to the north. You all decide to try to get there. Which way would you sail, and which direction is north?

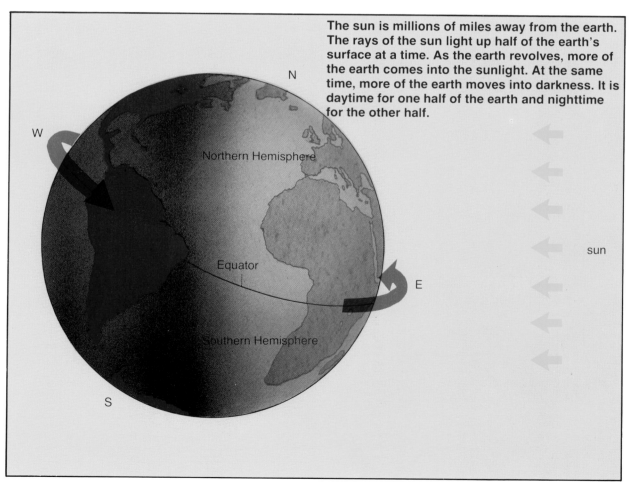

The sun is millions of miles away from the earth. The rays of the sun light up half of the earth's surface at a time. As the earth revolves, more of the earth comes into the sunlight. At the same time, more of the earth moves into darkness. It is daytime for one half of the earth and nighttime for the other half.

Luckily, the morning sun is shining. You watch its position changing in the sky. You can put a stick in the sand to see when the sun is at its highest. The **shadow** of the stick will get shorter and shorter. When it is at its shortest, it will be noon. The shadow will point north if you are in the Northern Hemisphere and south if you are in the Southern Hemisphere. Now, you know which way to sail.

Keeping on Course

Once you set sail, you have to know how to stay **on course**. This means sailing in the right direction all the time. The first sailors had no instruments, but you or one of your friends may have a watch with a dial. If it is working, you can use it to find north or south at any time between sunrise and sunset.

Point the small hour hand at the sun. North and south are then along the line halfway between the numeral 12 and the small hour hand. You can see from the picture how this works. Try it out for yourself sometime. **Remember not to look directly at the sun. It will damage your eyes**.

▼ You can use a wristwatch to find north and south whenever the sun is shining. Point the small hour hand toward the sun. Imagine a straight line halfway between the hour hand and the number 12 on the watch. That line points north and south.

North/South line

sun

North/South line

Signposts in the Sky

You can find the way by night if you can see the stars. If you look at the stars from the earth, they change their positions in the sky just like the sun. We cannot see a pattern in the way the stars move. In the Northern Hemisphere, the first sailors soon found out that there was a star that could help them.

The North Star

The sailors in the Northern Hemisphere could see that one star always appeared to stay in the same position. That star appears to stay still because it is directly over the North Pole. The star is therefore called the North Star, or Polaris. Its position never changes, and it always shows where north is.

The picture will help you to find the North Star. Look first for the group of stars, or **constellation**, called the Great Bear. Think of the Great Bear as a pot and find the "handle." Look across to the opposite side of the pot and you will find two stars. These stars point toward the North Star, which is brighter than the stars around it. It is easy to find in the night sky.

The Great Bear has other names. In the United States, the Great Bear is called the Dipper or the Big Dipper. A dipper is a kind of spoon, or ladle, which is used for serving food. In Britain, the Great Bear is sometimes called the Plough because its shape reminded people of an old plough (plow). The proper name for the Great Bear is *Ursa Major*. These are Latin words which mean "Greater Bear."

▼ **The Great Bear moves around the North Star throughout the night. It could be in any of these positions.**

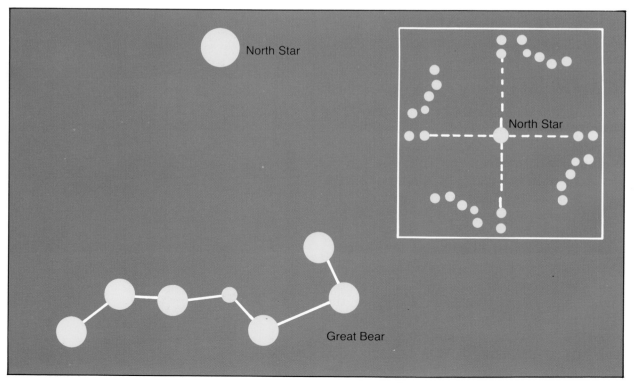

The Southern Cross

The discovery of the North Star made it easier for the sailors in the Northern Hemisphere to find their way at night. The sailors in the Southern Hemisphere were not so lucky. The North Star cannot be seen there.

In the Southern Hemisphere, there is a group of stars called the Southern Cross, or *Crux Australis*. This group gives a rough guide to find the direction south. There are 4 stars in the Southern Cross. They make a shape more like a kite than a cross. They stand out from the stars around them because they are so bright. They cannot be seen from North America or Europe.

▲ This photograph of the sky was taken at night over a long period of time. It shows that the stars appear to move around the North Star in a circle.

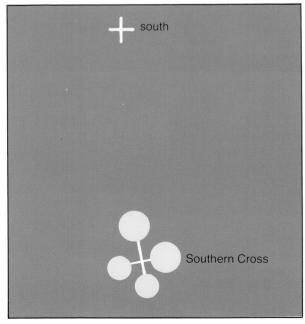

south

Southern Cross

► People who live in the Southern Hemisphere find south by using the Southern Cross. It is made up of four stars in the shape of a cross.

The First Surveyors

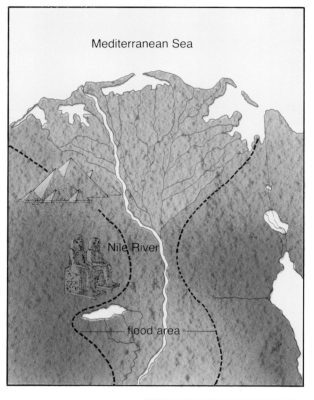

Mediterranean Sea

Nile River

flood area

Maps are made by **surveyors**. Surveyors measure the distances between places on the earth. They use these measurements to build up a picture of the land as it would appear if you looked down on it from an airplane.

Surveyors have to be very **accurate** in their work. They use special instruments to help them. The first surveyors worked out simple ways of measuring the land so that it could be divided up fairly.

The Ancient Egyptians

Some of the first skills of surveying were used in ancient Egypt about 4,000 years ago. Ancient Egypt was one of the first **civilizations**. It grew up around the Nile River.

Each year, the Nile flooded at the same time. The flood water spread over the land on either side of the river. The land was then ready for the grain to be planted. First, however, the land had to be divided up between the farmers. The good farmers received the most land. The priests of ancient Egypt made the owners of each strip of land pay **taxes**. They had to know how much land each person farmed.

▲ The ancient Egyptians lived beside the Nile River. Some of their building and surveying methods are still in use today.

▶ The ancient Egyptians built burial tombs for their kings and queens. The Great Pyramid near Cairo was one of the seven great wonders of the world. It was built of stone blocks on a square base. Each pyramid came to a point at the top.

▶ The Egyptians made a right angle with a loop of rope. Around the loop there were 12 evenly-spaced knots. They arranged the loop on the ground to make a triangle. The angle opposite the side with five spaces was a right angle. The other two sides had three spaces and four spaces. Two triangles made in this way could be fitted together to make one rectangle.

Measuring the Land

The easiest way to divide the land was to mark it out in strips. Each strip was made in the shape of a **rectangle**. The four sides of each rectangle could be measured easily because each side was a straight line. Also, the surveyors could figure out the **area** or the amount of land. To do this they multiplied the length of the long side of the rectangle by the length of the short side.

The surveyors used a length of knotted rope to make the measurements. A knot was tied at every **cubit**. An Egyptian cubit was about half a yard long. The knotted rope was also used to make a **right angle** at each of the corners of the rectangle.

Making Buildings

The ancient Egyptians built huge stone **tombs** which we call **pyramids**. They also built many beautiful palaces and temples. They had to be able to measure accurately to make these buildings.

The temple walls had to be straight and upright. To accomplish this, the surveyors used a **plumb line** — a length of string with a weight on the end. The weight made the string hang down in a straight line along the side of a wall. The surveyor could then see if the wall was crooked. Builders and surveyors still use a plumb line today.

▶ The Egyptians used a plumb line to check that the walls of their buildings were exactly upright. One man held the line while the other man checked with his eye that it was hanging straight and the stone blocks were upright.

Making Plans

Maps and **plans** are used to show what land and objects look like as if you were looking down on them from above. The ancient Egyptians made plans of their buildings, but they did not draw them on paper. Instead, they drew the first small plan of a building by scratching it with a stick on sand. Then the surveyors drew the plan out full size on the piece of ground where the temple was to be built.

Seen from Above

It is not always easy to recognize an object by looking at its plan. A picture of a round table with four legs would be easy to recognize. The plan of the table, however, would be just an outline in the form of a circle. That circle could also be the plan of a plate, or a ball, or even of the full moon seen from the earth.

If you stand in front of a house and draw what you see, it will be only part of the house. The same house will look different from above. You will see the roof and the ground around the house. This is called a plan view.

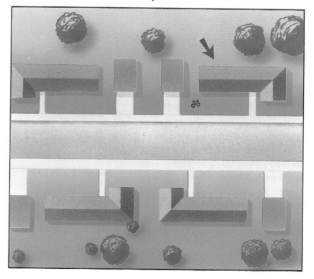

The Floor Plan of a House

The picture on the opposite page tells you a lot about the outside of the house. It shows you where the windows and the front door are. The picture does not, however, tell you how many rooms there are or how they fit together inside the house. You would need to see a **floor plan** to find this out. A floor plan shows how the house would look from above if the roof were taken off. If a house has more than one floor, there has to be a floor plan for each floor.

Making a Plan of a Room

See if you can make a floor plan of the room you are in. You will need a pencil and some graph paper. Use your feet to measure each side of the room. Place your heel against one of the walls. Then, walk forward, putting the heel of one foot very close to the toe of the other foot. Do this all the way across the room. Count the paces as you go forward.

The number of paces gives you the length of one side of the room as a number of paces. Now, do the same thing for each of the other sides. Write down the number of paces for each of the sides.

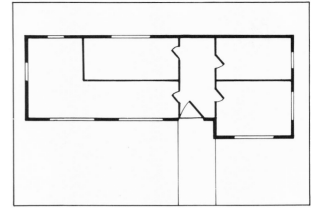

▲ The floor plan shows the house seen from above with the roof removed. The plan shows the size and number of rooms. It also shows where the doors and windows are.

Next, count the number of squares on the longest side of the graph paper. Are there enough squares to take the number of paces on the longest side of the room? If not, then make each square stand for two or more paces so that the plan can fit on the paper.

When you have figured this out, draw the floor plan of the room on the graph paper. Each square must stand for the same number of paces on each side of the plan.

▶ When you make a floor plan of a room, you put in as much detail as possible. You show where the windows, doors, and heating are. Then, you put in the chairs and tables, as though you were looking at them from above.

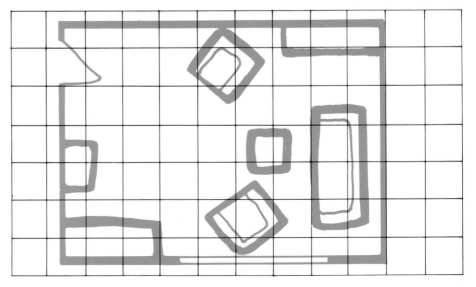

13

Using Magnets

Magnetite is a brownish rock with iron in it. Magnetite has special powers. The iron made from it is **magnetic**. If a piece of this iron is tied around the middle with string and allowed to swing freely, it will turn until the ends point north and south.

About 1,000 years ago, sailors began to use **magnets** to make **compasses**. The needle of a compass always points north and south. You can use it to figure out which way you want to go.

▲ This picture shows the four points of the compass, North, East, South, and West.

Making a Magnetic Needle

If you have a bar magnet, you can magnetize a needle. Then, you can make a simple compass. Using the bar magnet, stroke the needle in one direction for 30 seconds. Lift the magnet from the needle after each stroke. Now, test the needle to see if it has become magnetized. See if the needle will pick up a pin.

Making a Needle Compass

Now you are ready to make your compass. You will need a drinking straw, a saucer or shallow dish, and the magnetized needle.

Put a dot on the rim of the saucer with a felt tip pen. Put another dot exactly opposite the first. Now make two more dots, equally spaced between the other

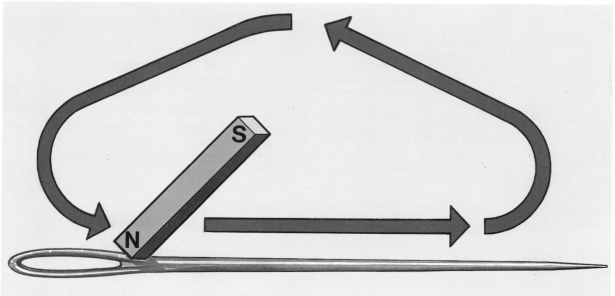

Using a bar magnet to magnetize a needle.

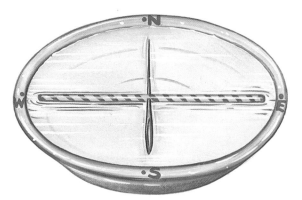

side of the needle so that the "cross" will float easily in the water. Float the needle and watch what happens. The needle will swing until it comes to rest in one position.

The needle will be pointing north and south. But which is which? Think of where the sun is at noon. That is south. If you live in the Southern Hemisphere, it is north. Turn the saucer carefully so that the S dot is in the south, and the needle is pointing at the N dot.

two. Write N for North against one of the dots and S for South against the opposite one. The dot on the right, between N and S, is E for East, and the opposite one is W for West.

Push the magnetized needle carefully through the center of the straw. It will make a cross. Now, put a little water in the saucer. Cut the straw short enough on each

Magnetic North

If you followed the N point on your compass, you would end up near the North Pole at a point called magnetic north. This is not the same place as the North Pole. The North Pole is a spot at the very top of the world. Magnetic north moves about. You can see below why this happens.

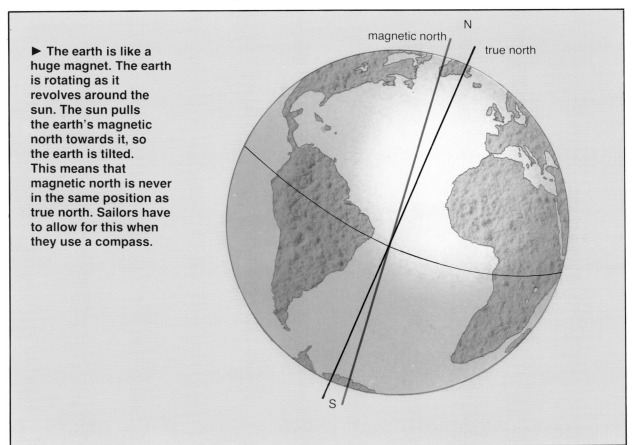

▶ The earth is like a huge magnet. The earth is rotating as it revolves around the sun. The sun pulls the earth's magnetic north towards it, so the earth is tilted. This means that magnetic north is never in the same position as true north. Sailors have to allow for this when they use a compass.

The First Charts

Every voyage was an adventure in the early days of sailing. Ships always tried to stay in sight of land because it was very easy to get lost away from the coasts. No one really knew how far one country was from another country. A journey might take only a day or two if the wind was in the right direction. When there was no wind, or when the wind was in the wrong direction, a voyage might last a week or more.

Keeping Records

The use of the magnetic compass made a great difference to travelers. Now, there was a way of recording, or **plotting**, the course a ship had taken. Captains began to keep records of their voyages. They wrote down details of sandbars and rocks wherever they sailed. They began to build up a picture of the seas and the coastlines.

The best way to show all this information was on **charts**. Charts are maps of the sea areas. The first charts were drawn on a material called **vellum**, which was made from calfskin. Copies of the charts were made and sold to other captains.

Mediterranean Lands

The Mediterranean Sea was once the busiest part of the world for shipping. The first charts were drawn of its coasts and islands. Later, charts of the seas around northern Europe were made.

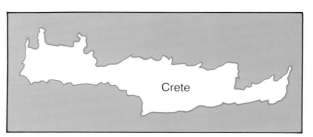

Crete

▶ This map of the island of Crete in the Mediterranean Sea was drawn by an Italian sailor in 1485. Compare it with the modern map. You can see that the old map was not very accurate. The old map was also upside down. The north part of the island is on the south side of the old map.

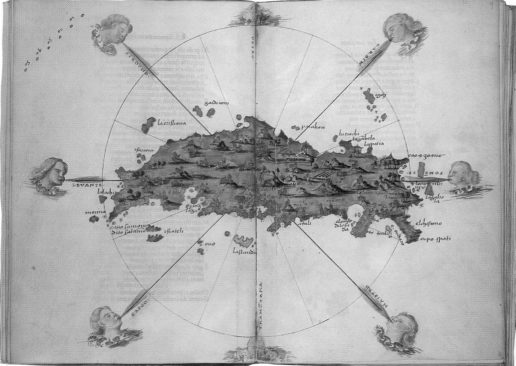

16

The coastlines on these old charts look very different from those shown on charts today. This was because there was no good way to measure distance at sea. Strong winds or **currents** might make the distance between two places seem longer than it really was. As more charts were made, they became more accurate.

Charting the Oceans

About 500 years ago, explorers began to sail out into the great oceans. They sailed across the Atlantic and the Pacific Oceans.

Then, in 1519, Ferdinand Magellan set sail from Spain on the greatest voyage of all. He sailed all the way around the world.

No one could have made any of these journeys without the help of the compass. The explorers brought back charts of the coasts they had seen. These were the first charts of the great oceans of the world.

▲ These ship's instruments were used 400 years ago. The instrument on the left was used to find the height of the sun. On the right is a ship's compass and a lump of magnetite in a brass box.

▼ This chart of the Atlantic is over 400 years old. North America is shown on the top left, with Europe and Africa on the right.

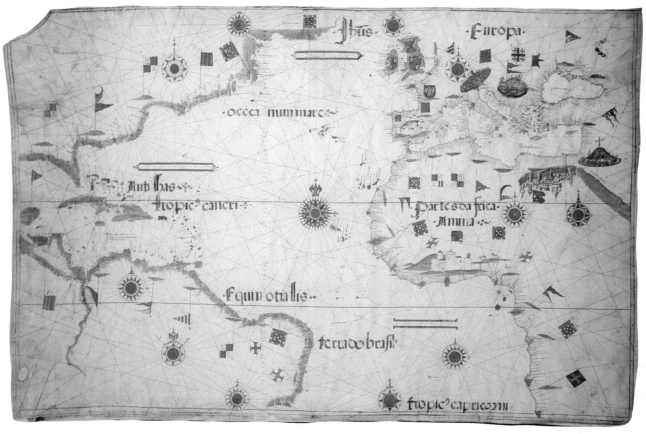

The Height of the Sun

The earth turns around once every 24 hours. As the earth rotates, the sun appears to rise, climb into the sky, and then set. It reaches its highest point in the sky at noon. However, it is the earth that is moving and not the sun. The sun at noon is nearly overhead in countries near the Equator. Near the North and South Poles, however, the sun never gets far above the **horizon**. The early sailors noticed that the height of the sun varied as they went north or south.

By measuring the height of the sun, they could figure out how far north or south of the Equator they were.

Latitude

Latitudes are imaginary lines which go around the world from east to west. The latitude around the middle of the world is the Equator. All other latitudes are named as being north or south of the Equator. The latitude of the Equator is 0 **degrees**. The latitude of the North Pole is 90 degrees north. The South Pole is 90 degrees south. Latitudes are sometimes called **parallels**.

▼ This picture was taken in Greenland. It shows the highest point the sun ever reaches there.

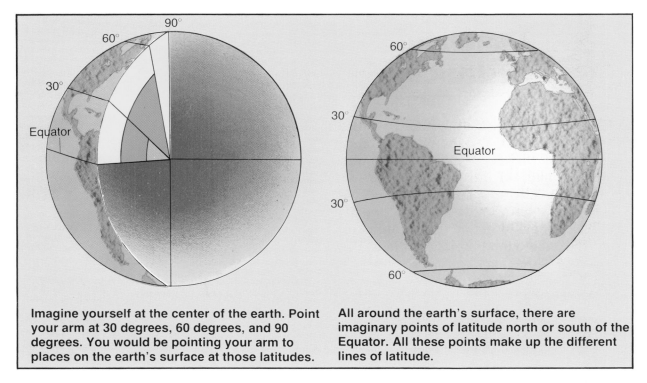

Imagine yourself at the center of the earth. Point your arm at 30 degrees, 60 degrees, and 90 degrees. You would be pointing your arm to places on the earth's surface at those latitudes.

All around the earth's surface, there are imaginary points of latitude north or south of the Equator. All these points make up the different lines of latitude.

Angles and Degrees

The number of degrees of latitude stands for an **angle**. Imagine that you are standing on level ground, such as the floor of a house. Stretch your arm out straight in front of you so that it is parallel with the ground. Your arm is at an angle of 0 degrees to the ground. Now, raise your arm until it is pointing straight upwards. Your arm is now at an angle of 90 degrees to the ground. If you raised your arm halfway between the two, it would be at an angle of 45 degrees.

Measuring Instruments

Sailors figure out their latitude by measuring the angle between the sun and the horizon at noon. At one time, they used an instrument called a **backstaff** to do this. The backstaff was hard to use unless the sea was calm. Later, a better instrument called a **sextant** was invented.

A sextant is really two **telescopes**. One is fixed, and the other can be moved. A sailor using a sextant points the fixed part at the horizon. Then, the sailor moves the other part to find the sun. Mirrors bring the sun into view. Next, the instrument is moved until the sun seems to "sit" on the horizon. Degrees marked on the sextant give the angle between the sun and the horizon. This is the same as the latitude north or south of the Equator. Sextants are still used on board ship today.

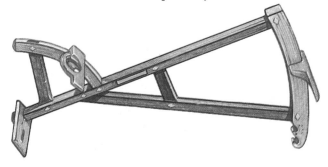

▲ The backstaff was invented in 1594. Sailors used it to measure the height of the sun. They lined up the top arm of the backstaff with the sun and the lower arm with the horizon.

Time and Distance

The people who sailed around the world 500 years ago had a sextant to figure out their latitude. They also had the compass to show them the direction in which they were sailing. This gave them their course. Then, they had to know how far they had sailed each day. Without this information, they did not know exactly where they were, and how far they were from the land.

► Sailors used the log and line to measure the distance a ship traveled. They threw the log and line into the sea. They counted the knots on the line as it slipped through their hands.

▼ Sailors used an hourglass to measure time before clocks were invented.

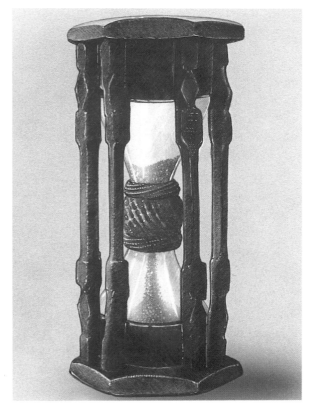

Log and Line

A ship's captain had to know how fast his ship was sailing. To find the ship's speed an hourglass and a log and line were used. The hourglass was like an egg timer. It was a glass, pinched in the middle, with sand inside. The sand took a fixed time to fall from the top half of the glass to the bottom half. The log was a heavy piece of wood which had been soaked well in water. The line was a long cord which was tied to the log. There were knots at regular intervals along the line.

The log was thrown overboard, and, at the same moment, the hourglass was turned over. The line was let out, and the log stayed in one place as the ship sailed on. A sailor counted the knots as they slipped through his hands. At the same time, the sand trickled into the bottom half of the hourglass. When all the sand had trickled through, the sailor stopped counting the knots and pulled in the line.

The captain was able to figure out the speed of his ship from the number of knots the sailor had counted and the number of minutes from the hourglass. Since the captain knew the direction he was sailing by the compass, he could now figure out roughly where he was in the ocean. This method of figuring out a ship's position was known as **dead reckoning**.

The log and line are no longer used, but sailors still use words that date from those days. The diary of a ship's voyage is still called the **logbook**. Speed at sea is still measured in **knots**.

The Chronometer

Dead reckoning was not a safe method to use on the ocean. Too many ships were lost at sea. In 1714, the British Navy offered a prize for an accurate clock to be used in ships. The prize was won by an Englishman, John Harrison. He called his clock a **chronometer**. After six weeks at sea, Harrison's chronometer was only five seconds off the correct time. With this accurate way of measuring time, sailors could find out how far east or west they were after leaving port. On the next page, you will find out how this is done.

▶ John Harrison's chronometer was made in 1735. This large clock kept accurate time in a rolling ship at sea. It also worked well in any temperature. With clocks like this, ships were able to work out longitude at any time of the day or night.

Accurate Navigation

The sextant gives a ship its latitude, north or south. The chronometer gives the ship a position east or west. This is called the **longitude**. When we know the latitude and longitude of a place, we know its exact position.

Longitude

Lines of longitude go around the world from north to south. They are not parallel to each other like the lines of latitude. They are like the lines that divide the pieces of orange inside the peel. They are wide apart at the Equator and get closer until they all meet at the North and South Poles. These imaginary lines are sometimes called **meridians**.

The Prime Meridian

One of these meridians goes through Greenwich, near London, England. It is called the Prime Meridian. This line is 0 degrees longitude. All other longitudes are named as being east or west of Greenwich. Everywhere in the world that lies on the Prime Meridian has the same time. It is called Greenwich Mean Time, or GMT.

Along the Prime Meridian, the sun will be at its highest point in the sky at noon everywhere. As a ship travels east or west of the Prime Meridian, the time changes. For every 15 degrees of longitude, the time changes by one hour. To the west of Greenwich, it is one hour earlier, and to the east of Greenwich, it is one hour later.

▼ To find the exact position of a place on the earth, you need to know two things. The first thing is the number of degrees north or south of the Equator (latitude). The second thing is the number of degrees east or west of the Prime Meridian (longitude).

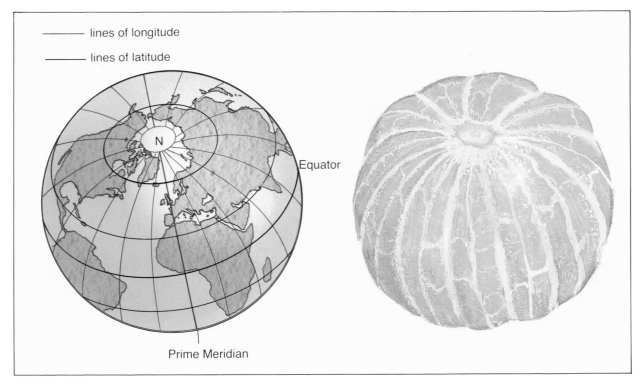

lines of longitude
lines of latitude
Equator
Prime Meridian

A ship's captain has to know two kinds of time, the GMT or the time at Greenwich, and local time, which is the time at the place where the ship is. The captain can find out the local time by using the sextant. The ship's chronometer keeps Greenwich Mean Time. The difference between the two times shows how far west or east the ship is.

Time Signals

Ships still have chronometers on board, but they do not need them if the radio is working. Radio stations all over the world send out time signals each hour. These signals are usually in the form of "pips." These pips are short bursts of sound. They sometimes end with a longer pip on the hour. Ships can use these time signals to check GMT.

Whole numbers of degrees only give a ship a rough position. For a more accurate position, one degree can be broken down into 60 minutes. Each minute can be broken into 60 seconds. A position given in seconds, anywhere in the world, is accurate to within about 30 yards.

▲ The Shepherd 24-hour clock was put in place at Greenwich in 1852. At that time, it was the most accurate clock in the world.

◄ The Prime Meridian, or 0 degree line, can be seen at Greenwich near London. This line was agreed as the Prime Meridian at Washington D.C., in 1884.

Using a Grid

The lines of latitude and longitude make a crisscross pattern that covers the map of the whole world. This pattern is called a **grid**. The maps on these pages have grids too, but they are more simple ones. The squares going across the map have letters. The squares going down have numbers. You can put a letter and a number together to point out one particular square. This is called a **grid reference**. Look at the map below. What can you see in grid reference E3?

Which Way?

When you use a map, you have to know where you are. You also have to know where you want to go. In the map below, you will see your home and your friend's home. Your home is in one position on the map. Your friend's home is in another position. The map will show the best way to get there.

Suppose you had to explain to some people how to get to your friend's home. If you had a map like this one, you could say, "There is my home in grid reference E5. When you come out of the gate, turn left and go on until you come to a road junction. Then, turn right. Soon, you will come to the bridge in C3. After that, there is another road junction. Keep going

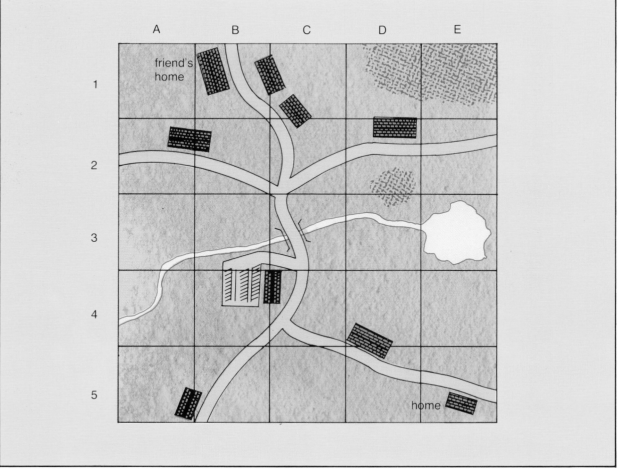

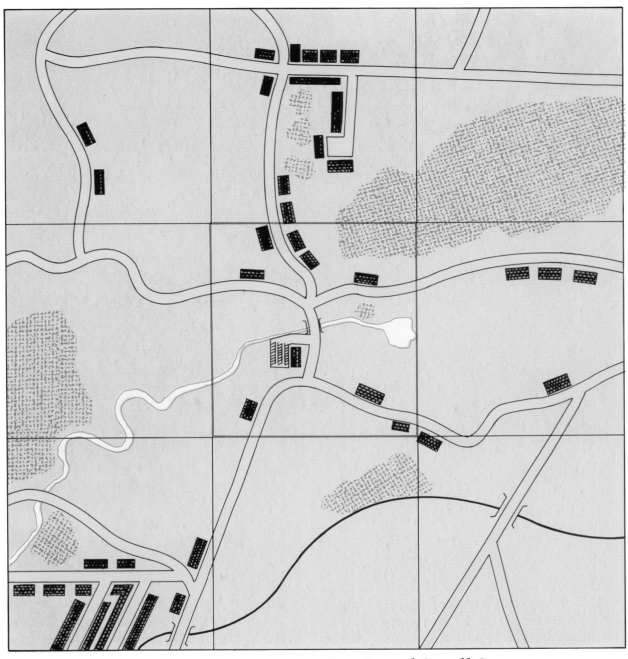

straight. Go past the houses on the right side of the street. Then you will see my friend's home on the left in B1."

You could give directions for this short journey without using a map, but the map makes it easier. If someone got lost, the map could show the way to your friend's home.

Large and Small Squares

Every map has a **scale**. Each square on the map stands for a far larger square of real land. In the first map, each square **represents** one square mile of land. In the second map, each square represents five square miles of land. The second map is on a smaller scale, but it shows more land.

25

Looking at Maps

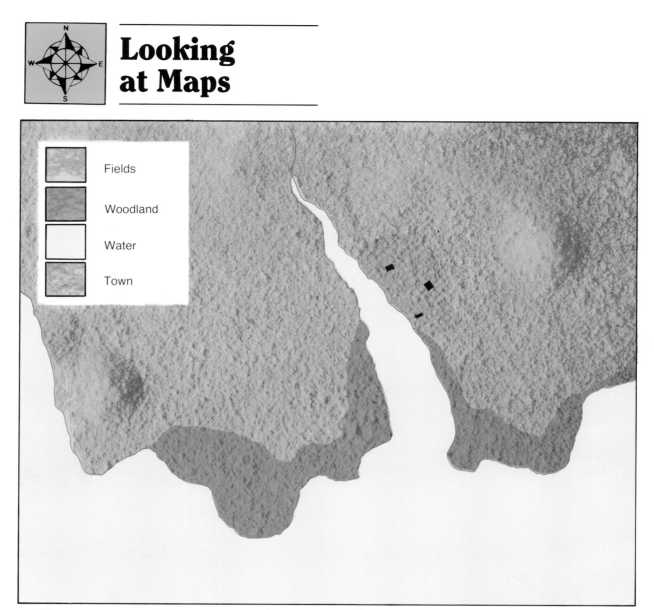

Fields	
Woodland	
Water	
Town	

There are many different types of maps. Large-scale maps show the most detail. These maps show a small area of land. Large-scale maps are the most accurate maps. They show every street and alleyway in a city. A map on this scale would be of little use to drivers. They need smaller scale maps which show a larger area of land, because they travel more quickly. Drivers need maps which show a number of towns and cities and the roads between them.

An even smaller scale is needed to show a whole country on one map. A map showing the whole world would have a scale so small that only the largest countries could be seen easily. Sometimes, maps are bound together as books. These books of maps are called **atlases**. A road atlas is a collection of maps for drivers. A world atlas is a collection of maps of different countries. In these atlases, the scale may be different from one map to another.

Using Colors

Most maps and atlases are printed in color. The use of color makes them easier and more interesting to read. Rivers, ponds, lakes, seas, and oceans are usually colored blue. Green is often used for fields and forests. Towns and cities are shown in red on many maps, although black is sometimes used.

There are no rules about the colors used on maps, but most map makers use the same colors for the same things. There is one way to find out what the colors on a map mean. Most maps have a **key** or **legend**, which is a kind of color code. The key is usually printed on the bottom or on the side of the map. In an atlas, it is usually found on a page at the beginning. The key tells you what the colors mean. Keys and legends help you to understand maps.

Road and Rail

The key may also tell you how roads and railroads are marked. On road maps, it is important to know which roads are the best to use. Green is used for interstate highways. Other main roads are often red. Black is used for less important roads. Very narrow "backroads" are often shown in blue. Railroad lines are usually printed in black.

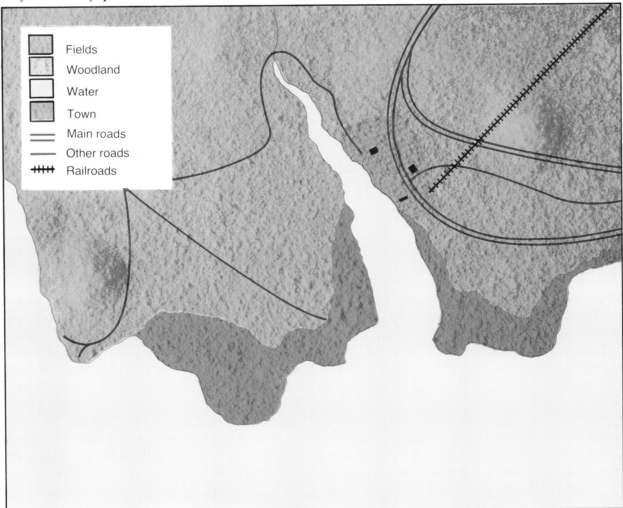

	Fields
	Woodland
	Water
	Town
	Main roads
	Other roads
	Railroads

Depths and Heights

Different colors and shades are often used on maps to show the height of the land and the depth of the sea. Ships' captains have to know the depth of water beneath their ships at all times. Airplane pilots and climbers need to know the height of mountains. Maps that show height or **elevation** and depth are called **physical** or **relief** maps. Look at a relief map in your atlas.

Heights and depths are measured above and below **sea level**. This is the level that the sea reaches halfway between low and high tides. If we say that a hill is 1,000 feet high, we mean that the top is 1,000 feet above sea level.

How Deep?

The ups and downs of the land do not stop where the land meets the sea. There are ups and downs under the sea. Maps usually show the depth of the sea in white and shades of blue. The white section shows the shallow water. The darkest shade of blue shows the deepest sea.

Near the coast, the sea is usually no more than about 135 yards deep. Out in the ocean, it is much deeper. The deepest ocean in the world is the Pacific. In one place south of Japan, it is about 6 miles deep. This very deep part is called the Marianas Trench.

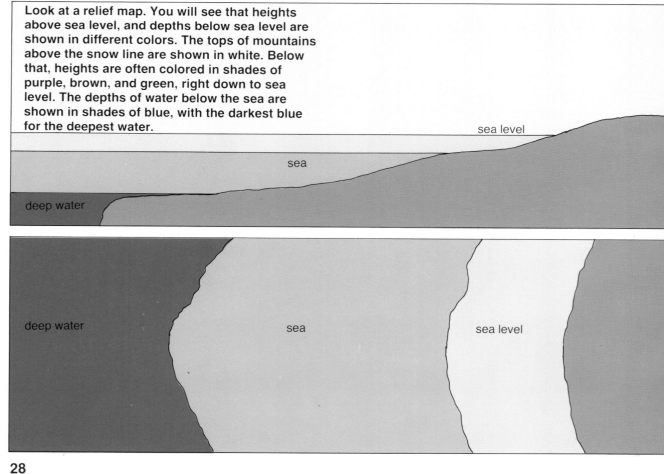

Look at a relief map. You will see that heights above sea level, and depths below sea level are shown in different colors. The tops of mountains above the snow line are shown in white. Below that, heights are often colored in shades of purple, brown, and green, right down to sea level. The depths of water below the sea are shown in shades of blue, with the darkest blue for the deepest water.

How High?

The height of land above sea level is also shown on relief maps by bands of color. Low-lying land is often shown in bluish-green. Slightly higher land is in a lighter green. Then, as the land gets even higher, there are shades of brown. Mountains are often purple. White is used often for the very highest mountain **peaks** to show where snow lies all the year round.

Not all map makers use the same colors. On the map, or on a page in your atlas, you will find a legend. This will show you the colors used for the different heights and depths. It will also show you the heights and depths at which the colors change. Always look for the legend. It will help you to read and understand the map.

mountain peak

low-lying land

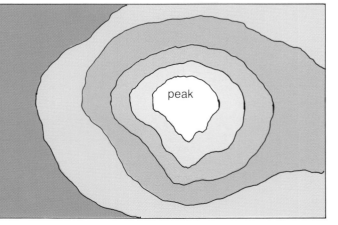

low-lying land

peak

Maps of
the World

▼ If you look at the top of a globe, you can see North America, Greenland, and Northern Europe. The size and shape of the countries on a globe are accurate since the globe is round like the earth itself.

◀ With this projection, you can see most of the world. However, the countries are not so accurate as they are on the globe. Greenland is shown far larger than it should be.

The world is shaped like a ball. It is a **sphere**. Look at a map of the world in an atlas. A map of the world does not look round because it is printed flat on paper.

Imagine cutting a beach ball into pieces and trying to stick them down flat on a piece of paper. It would be very difficult. Map makers have to try to show something that is round on a flat surface.

Looking at a Globe

The best idea you can get of the world is to look at a globe. You can make it rotate in just the same way as the earth turns. You can see the exact direction you would have to take to get from one place to another. A globe gives an accurate picture of the world.

You could not, however, carry a globe around with you wherever you went. A map or atlas is easier to use. If you want to look at all the countries of the world at the same time, you can only do so by looking at a map.

Mapping the World

Map makers partly solve the problem of turning something round into something flat. They use **projections**. These are ways of making the curved surface of the earth look flat. In the map on page 30, all the lines of longitude are straight. You know this is not correct. Lines of longitude all meet at the poles. Therefore, in that projection, the north and south edges of the map have been "stretched" to cover the page. This makes Greenland look almost as big as Africa. Actually, Africa is about 14 times the size of Greenland.

The map below is more accurate. Greenland looks nearer to its true size. The lines of longitude come closer together at the poles, but they do not meet. No map can be as accurate as a globe.

▼ With this projection you can see the whole world on one map. It is more accurate than the projection on the left because it is drawn more like a globe.

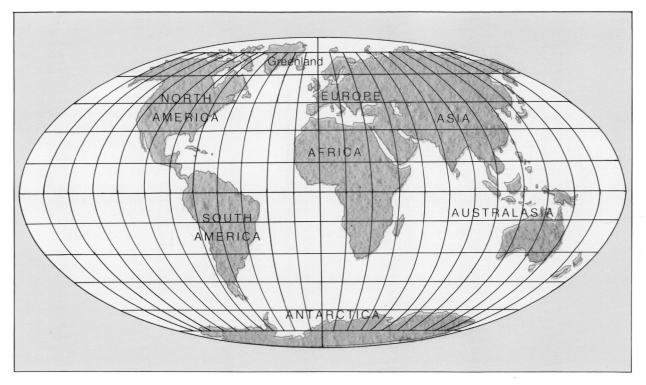

The World from Above

Until about 50 years ago, there was only one way to make maps. People had to walk over the ground and survey it. Some places were very difficult to map. Jungles and mountains could not be surveyed easily. It was even harder to survey deserts and swamps.

Photographs from the Air

Airplanes have made it easier to map places that are hard to get at. An air survey plane carries a camera that points straight down to the ground. The pilot may have to wait until the weather is clear. The air has to be still, and there must be no clouds. The plane must fly in a straight line over the land to be mapped. The pilot takes a **series** of photographs, one after another. Each picture **overlaps** the last one.

After the flight, the pictures are printed. They are put together like a jigsaw puzzle to make a **mosaic**. Then, a map is drawn from the mosaic. It is quicker and easier to make a map this way than it is to do a survey on the ground.

Ancient Buildings

Sometimes, the air photographs produce a surprise. Pictures taken from above often show things that cannot be seen from the ground. One photograph may show a faint outline where there was once a building hundreds of years ago. Signs of ancient farms and towns have often been found in this way. Then people who are interested in history dig carefully on the ground to unearth the remains of these farms and towns.

◄ This aerial photograph shows a part of the town of Farnham in southern England. The plane was about 3,000 feet above the ground. The photograph was taken at an angle and gives a side view of the buildings. This photo could not be used for making a map because the camera was not pointing straight down.

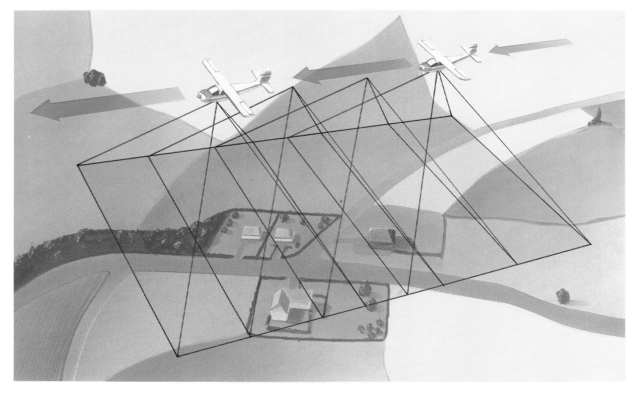

▲ The pilot has to fly over the land to be mapped in a straight line at a fixed height. The photos are taken one after the other to make a series. Then, they are placed together to make a total picture.

The World from Space

Space **satellites** can also be used to help make world maps. These satellites are put into an **orbit** around the earth. As they pass over land that needs to be surveyed, a television camera is switched on. The pictures are then sent back to earth. A satellite may be hundreds of miles up in space. Even from this height, the pictures are so clear that every building can be seen.

Pictures from satellites give map makers an up-to-date view of the whole earth. They show any changes that are taking place and can also show what is happening from day to day. There are special satellites that watch the weather. People use the photographs they take to forecast the weather.

▼ This photograph was taken from a satellite high above the earth. It shows the Nile Delta. Find the Nile Delta in an atlas and compare the two pictures.

Bird Navigators

We need maps and instruments to help us find our way around the world. Many birds, however, can find their way without any of these aids. All through the year, millions of birds are on the move. They know when to start off and which way to go. Some birds, such as swallows and swifts, return each year to nest in the same house or barn.

We are not sure how birds and animals find their way. They seem to be born with special skills which we do not have. If the skies are cloudy, birds often lose their way. This has led some people to think that birds find their way by using the sun and the stars to guide them.

Carrier Pigeons

Pigeons are very good at finding their way. They can be taken hundreds of miles away and will find their way back home. They have a **homing instinct**. Years ago, pigeons were used to carry messages. The message was rolled up and put into a small tube attached to the bird's leg.

Army commanders used pigeons to send orders to their troops in this way. This was often the only way to send messages, if troops were surrounded by the enemy.

Homing pigeons are still used in the sport of pigeon racing in Britain. The birds are all kept in a pigeon loft. Before the race, they are taken some distance away from the loft and set free. The first pigeon home wins the race.

▼ Each pigeon has its own nesting place in this old pigeon loft. Pigeons return home to the loft through a hole in the roof.

The Arctic Tern

The bird that makes the longest flight each year is the Arctic tern. This seabird breeds in summer in the north of Europe, Asia and America. The young birds grow quickly. As soon as they are fully grown, the terns set off in small groups. They fly thousands of miles over the sea until they reach the Antarctic. When they get there, it is spring in the Southern Hemisphere. The terns stay there for the summer and then fly north again. The round trip from north to south and back again is almost 11,000 miles!

Arctic terns nest and breed in North America, northern Europe, and Greenland, around the Arctic Ocean. As winter approaches, they fly south with their young to the coasts of the Southern Hemisphere, not far from the ice of the Antarctic Ocean. As winter approaches in the Southern Hemisphere, they fly back to the Arctic to breed.

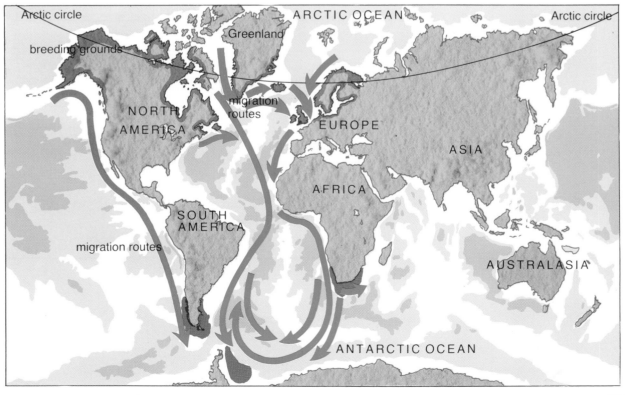

Arctic circle

ARCTIC OCEAN

Arctic circle

Greenland

breeding grounds

migration routes

NORTH AMERICA

EUROPE

ASIA

AFRICA

SOUTH AMERICA

migration routes

AUSTRALASIA

ANTARCTIC OCEAN

Using Echoes

Have you ever shouted inside a large, empty building? If so, you may have heard your voice come back to you. You heard the **echo** of your voice. The sound of your voice hits the walls and bounces back. You hear the echo after you have shouted. It takes time for the sound to travel to the walls and back again to your ears.

Sound

Sound travels at about 750 mph or about 1,100 feet per second. In a thunderstorm, you see the lightning first. Then, a few seconds later, you hear the thunder. It takes aboout five seconds for the sound of thunder to travel one mile. If you hear the thunder five seconds after you see the lightning, it means that the storm is about one mile away.

▲ The horseshoe bat sends out high-pitched squeaks as it flies. The bat's large ears receive the sound back as echoes. This way the bat can avoid objects and catch insects to feed on.

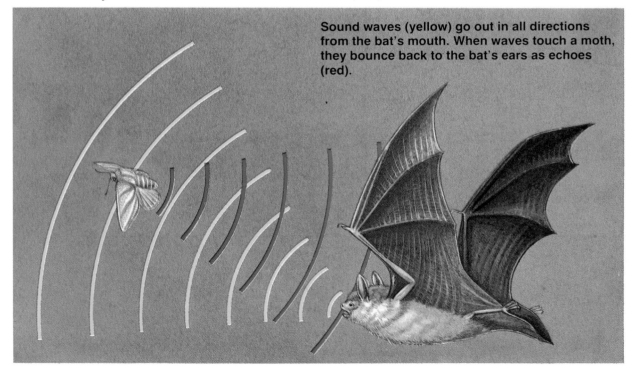

Sound waves (yellow) go out in all directions from the bat's mouth. When waves touch a moth, they bounce back to the bat's ears as echoes (red).

Bats

Most animals use their eyes to find their way around. Some animals, such as bats, have poor sight or none at all. They use their hearing to find their way.

Most of the large fruit eating bats have good sight, but the insect eating bats are almost blind. As bats fly, they send out a series of fast, highpitched squeaks. These sounds are too highpitched for most people to hear, but children can sometimes hear them.

The squeaks bounce off anything in the bat's way and the bat's big ears pick up the echo. The echo tells the bat when to turn or dive to avoid something. Because the echoes also bounce off insects in the air, the bat knows where to find its food. This method of finding the way is called **echolocation**.

Dolphins

Dolphins use echolocation to find their way. They are not blind, but their sight is poor. Instead of sending out squeaks like bats, dolphins send out a series of clicks and listen for the echoes. In this way, a dolphin can find the position of very small objects. Different objects send back different kinds of echo. The dolphin can tell whether the clicks have hit something soft like a fish or something hard like a rock.

The clicks which dolphins make cannot be heard by people. However, if the clicks are recorded on tape and played back fast, they can be heard.

▼ River dolphins have poor eyesight. They locate the small fish and shrimp they feed on by sending out clicks.

Sonar and Radar

We have taken some of our ideas for finding the way from nature. Echolocation is just one of these ideas. Bats and dolphins use echolocation. Planes and ships can also use echolocation in much the same way. There are two kinds of echolocation. One kind uses sound waves which travel at 750 mph. The other kind uses radio waves which move much faster. Radio waves travel at over 670,000,000 mph. They travel as fast as the speed of light — about 186,000 miles per second.

Sonar

Sonar is a way of finding out what is under the surface of the sea. It is an **acronym** which stands for **SO**und **NA**vigation **R**anging. "Ranging" means finding the distance. Sonar uses sound waves. Ships can use it to find out how deep the sea is. Sound waves are sent out from a ship into the water. If there is nothing in the way, the sound waves hit the ocean floor and bounce back. The time that the sound takes to come back shows how far down the ocean floor is. If there are fish beneath the water, the sound bounces off them. Then, it comes back more quickly, and fishermen know where to find shoals of fish. In wartime, sonar is used to find enemy submarines.

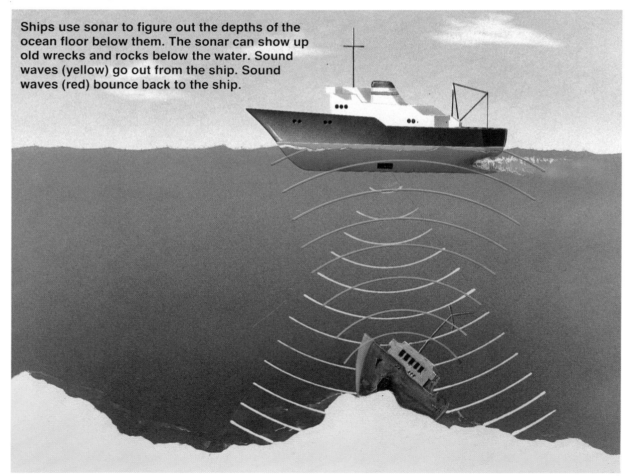

Ships use sonar to figure out the depths of the ocean floor below them. The sonar can show up old wrecks and rocks below the water. Sound waves (yellow) go out from the ship. Sound waves (red) bounce back to the ship.

Radar

Radar is another acronym. It stands for **RA**dio **D**etection **A**nd **R**anging, and it uses radio waves. It was first used during wartime to **detect** or find enemy planes and figure out how far away they were. Today, ships and airplanes depend upon radar for their safety.

There are two parts to a radar set. The first part sends out a stream of radio waves. These go out from a **scanner** which turns continuously through a complete circle. A **beam** of radio waves, or narrow band of sound, sweeps around the sky. If the waves meet anything like a plane, some waves bounce back.

These waves come back to the second part of the set. This is a screen like a television screen. It shows the plane as a "blip" or white spot. A large airplane makes a bigger blip than a small plane. The radar operator can see on the screen all the planes in the air near the radar station.

All large ships have radar. Their scanners sweep at sea level to pick up the coastline and other ships. The use of radar in fog and bad weather has made sea travel much safer.

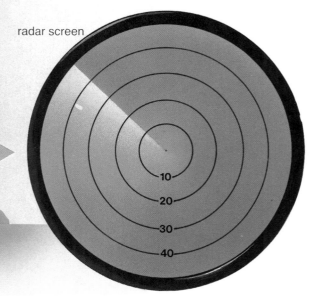

radar screen

radar scanner

The radar scanner sends out signals in all directions. When the signals meet a plane, echoes are bounced back. These echoes are shown as a blip of light on the radar screen.

Air Navigation

Airplane pilots have to know where they are and the direction in which they are flying. They must also keep out of each other's way. **Controllers** on the ground use radar to tell pilots how to avoid other planes.

Beacons

Once an airplane has taken off, it must obey the rules of the air. Each plane must fly along an air corridor. Air corridors are like main roads in the sky. Instead of lines and road signs, air corridors are marked by radio **beacons**. The beacons send out signals all the time. These signals are picked up on each plane's radio. The pilot has a map which shows where the beacons are. The pilot can use the signals and the map to find out exactly where the plane is. A controller tells the pilot how high the plane must fly as it passes each beacon.

As a plane nears the end of its flight, the pilot picks up a radio beam. If the plane stays on the beam, the pilot hears the sound all the time. If the plane strays off the beam, the sound changes. The beam helps the pilot to get the plane in the right position for landing.

There are **markers** at various points along the beam. These markers make different sounds. The pilot knows that at each marker the plane should be at a certain height. This helps the pilot to make a smooth approach and landing.

▼ The plane flies down a beam in the final approach. The marker is a radio signal beamed upwards. It tells the pilot that the plane is at the correct height.

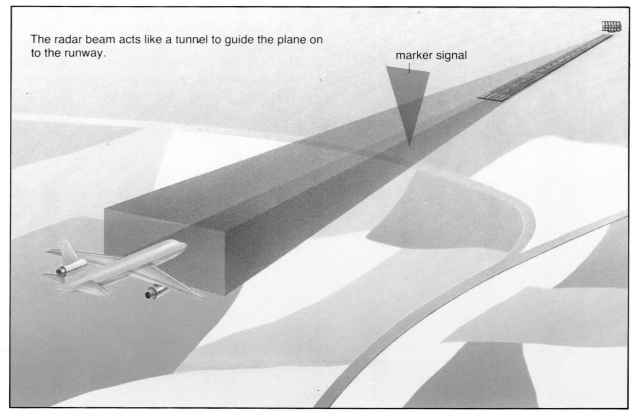

The radar beam acts like a tunnel to guide the plane on to the runway.

marker signal

► There are several controllers inside a radar station. The controllers can speak to the pilots by radio. Radar screens show where the planes are flying. Other screens show flight information.

▼ An airport radar scanner sends out radio waves. Waves bounce back when they meet a plane. The planes are shown as blips of light on the radar screen.

The Busy Skies

The sky around an airport is very busy. A number of planes are often waiting to land. They must not land until they are told to do so. The controller can see the movement of every plane on a radar screen. Captains are told by radio where to move next. The controller looks at the radar screen to check that the orders have been followed.

Transponders

How does the controller know which plane is which when there are several blips on the radar screen at the same time? Every plane carries a **transponder**. The transponder sends out the plane's **call-sign**. The call-sign shows on the radar screen beside the plane's own blip. This reduces the chance of the controller making a mistake.

There is another use for the transponder. If a blip disappears from the screen for some reason, the controller knows right away which plane is missing.

Ships at Sea

Today, almost every ship has radar. It is the law of the sea that all but the smallest ships must have radar. One of the greatest dangers at sea is fog. Before radar was invented, all that a ship could do in fog was to sound the foghorn and slow down. Everyone listened for the foghorns of other ships. In very thick fog, ships had to stop, or **heave to**, and wait for the fog to clear. Today, with radar, ships can sail on, although most ships still slow down in fog.

▼ Ships use radar to track the movements of other ships. This ship has two radar scanners high up on a mast. Some ships have scanners at either end.

A large ship has two radar scanners. There is one on the **bridge**, and another in the **wheelhouse**. They work in the same way as airport scanners. A beam of radio waves sweeps the sea. It bounces off other ships nearby. These show up as blips on the radar screen. As the blip moves, the course of the other ship can be plotted. The captain can then decide whether he has to alter course to avoid the other ship. The captains can talk to each other by radio when they have to.

Sea Lanes

There are some parts of the world where the seas are very busy. The English Channel between France and England is always full of ships. Ferry boats travel continuously back and forth between England and France. There are also large freighters and tankers sailing up and down the Channel between the Atlantic Ocean and the ports of northern Europe. Another busy sea lane is the entrance to the St. Lawrence Seaway in Canada.

▲ There are many different kinds of radar scanners. The large radar dome on this ship can detect planes as well as other ships.

In places like these, all ships are **radar-controlled** from the shore. They have to stay in separate sea lanes. These are like the lanes on a highway. Radar stations on shore check that the ships are keeping in their lanes. At the same time, each ship uses its own radar to watch for other ships in the area.

Using Satellites

Satellites are now used to help with navigation. They are launched by rockets and placed in orbit around the earth. Satellites can pick up messages from one part of the earth's surface and send them to another part of the earth. Icebergs are always a source of danger to ships in the North Atlantic. Satellites can watch these from space. Ships at sea can be told where the icebergs are so that they can alter course to avoid them. This helps ships entering and leaving northern ports or rivers such as the St. Lawrence Seaway.

Satellite Navigation

Satellites make it easy for a ship to figure out its position. Radar can be used close to the shore. Radar is a good aid over a short

When the Transit satellite is over the ship, a signal is picked up by the ship's receiver (1). The satellite moves on and another signal (2) is picked up. Transit moves on again and sends yet another signal (3). A computer on the ship measures the time and angle of the signals. From this the computer is able to figure out the accurate position of the ship. The ground station (4) controls the satellite.

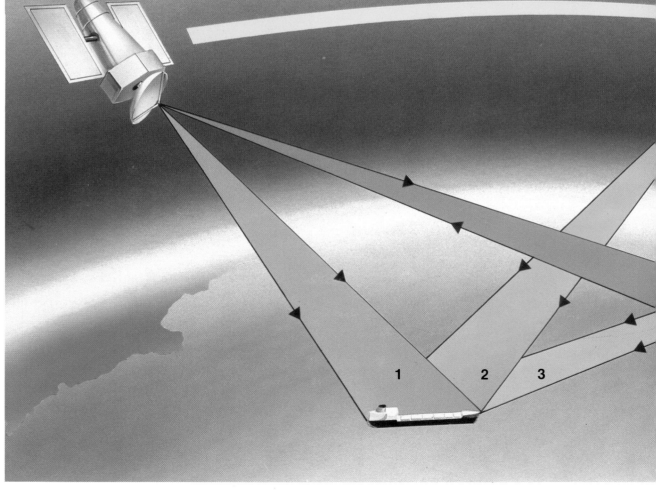

distance, but it cannot "see" over the horizon. Radar is no use for figuring out a ship's position out in the ocean.

Satellites are used in a system of navigation called "Transit." The Transit satellite sends out radio signals as it orbits around the earth. A receiver in the ship picks up these signals as Transit passes over. Transit moves on, and more signals are picked up on the ship. The time and the direction of the signals are different. From these signals, a computer on board figures out where the ship is. This is the most accurate way that has been found to fix the position of a ship at sea.

Communication Satellites

Communication satellites can keep ships in touch with the shore. They orbit in a different way from Transits. They are put into orbit at about 25,000 miles above the earth. At this height, it takes them 24 hours to go around the earth. This is the same time as it takes the earth itself to rotate once. Because of this, the satellite seems to stay in a fixed position. Ships and ground stations can bounce messages off the satellites. They can communicate with each other even if they are thousands of miles apart.

Finding the way by land, sea, and air today is no longer as difficult as it once was. Navigation is much more accurate, and is, therefore, much safer.

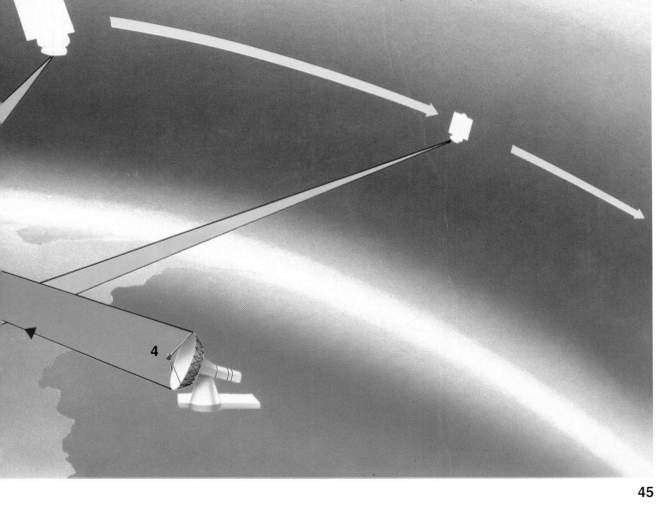

Glossary

accurate: exactly right, done with care. You must make accurate measurements when building a house or making a map.

acronym: a word made up from the first letters of the name of something. Radar is an acronym for **RA**dio **D**etection **A**nd **R**anging.

angle: the space between two lines which meet. Angles are measured in degrees.

area: the amount of something flat, like land, that can be measured.

atlas, -es: a book of maps. An atlas is named after a giant called Atlas in Greek mythology.

backstaff: an instrument used for measuring the height of the sun above the horizon. It was called a backstaff because the person using it stood with his back to the sun.

beacon: a signal which acts as a guide or a warning for ships and planes. Each beacon sends out a different signal so that sailors or pilots can determine their positions.

beam: a signal or ray of light sent out along a narrow path. A flashlight, or the headlights of a car send out light in the form of a beam.

bridge: the raised section from which the captain controls the ship.

call-sign: a special signal sent out by a plane so that controllers at busy airports can tell which plane it is. Every plane has a different call-sign.

chart: maps used by sailors. Charts show the depth of the water, the coastline, and special markers like lighthouses to help people find their way safely.

chronometer: a special clock which keeps very good time at sea. It is not affected by large changes in temperature or by the movement of ships.

civilization: a large organized group of people who have settled in one place to live. They have rules or laws about the way they live and behave.

communication satellite: an object that people have launched into space. It receives and passes on signals from the earth so that people can talk to each other when they are very far apart.

compass: an instrument that is used to find direction. It contains a needle which points north. The four points of the compass are N (North), S (South), E (East), and W (West).

constellation: a group of stars as they are seen from the earth.

controller: a person who directs people or machines to do something. Controllers at airports are in charge of the movements of aircraft.

cubit: an old measure of length. The length of the arm from the elbow to the tip of the middle finger.

current: the flow of water in a sea, ocean, or river.

dead reckoning: a rough method of figuring out where you are without using the sun and stars. It is based on working out the direction and distance you have traveled from your last known position.

degree: the unit of measurement of an angle. If you turn around once when you are standing on the ground, you will turn 360 degrees.

detect: to find out where something is.

direction: the course to take or the way to go to reach a point or place.

echo: a sound sent back to where it started. Echoes are caused by sounds bouncing off a hard object.

echolocation: a way of finding objects by sending out sound and then listening for the sound, or echo. Bats use echolocation to find their prey.

elevation: the height that something is above sea level.

Equator: an imaginary line which is drawn around the middle of the earth. The Equator divides the northern part of the earth from the southern part.

floor plan: a drawing to show the shape and measurements of a room on one floor of a building, as seen from above.

grid: a pattern of lines which makes squares on a map.

grid reference: a letter and number which show the exact position of a place on a map with a grid.

heave to: to stop a ship and then keep it in the same position.

hemisphere: a half of a sphere. A sphere is a round object. If it is cut in half, there are two hemispheres.

homing instinct: the natural ability of an animal to find its way home without thinking.

horizon: the distant line where the sky and the sea, or land appear to meet.

instinct: something that people or animals are born with that makes them behave in a certain way without thinking.

instrument: a tool made by people to help them do something. A sextant is an instrument which helps sailors figure out their positions at sea.

key: something which "unlocks" the meaning or explains what certain things stand for. The key of a map explains the meaning of the colors and the marks used on a map.

knot: a measure of speed of one sea mile per hour.

latitude: one of many imaginary lines drawn around the world from east to west and above or below the Equator. A position on the earth north or south of the Equator.

legend: another word for "key." The legend of a map explains the meaning of the colors and the marks used on a map.

logbook: the book kept in each ship in which details of a voyage are written down every day.

longitude: one of many imaginary lines drawn from the North Pole to the South Pole across the surface of the earth. A position on the earth east or west of the line of longitude running through Greenwich, England.

magnet: a piece of iron or steel that attracts other objects of iron or steel to it.

magnetic: having the power to attract.

magnetite: a rock containing a type of iron that attracts other things made of iron.

marker: a radio or light signal at points along the approach of a plane coming in to land.

meridian: another name for a line of longitude. It is one of many imaginary lines drawn from the North Pole to the South Pole across the surface of the earth.

migration: the movement of animals over long distances to find food, to produce young, or to escape from cold weather.

mosaic: a pattern, design, or picture made by fitting many small pieces together.

navigate: to find the way from one place to another place by using the sun and the stars, landmarks, and special instruments.

on course: going in the correct direction.

orbit: the path of one body, like a planet or a satellite, around another body. The earth moves in orbit around the sun.

overlap: to arrange something so that it partially covers something else.

parallel (*adj*): running side by side but staying the same distance apart.

parallel (*noun*): a line of latitude, which is one of the many imaginary lines drawn around the world from east to west.

peak: the pointed top of a mountain.

physical: having to do with the earth's natural areas such as mountains and oceans.

plan: a drawing to show the shape of something, such as a building, as seen from above.

plot, -ting: to mark on a map or chart the direction of a moving ship or aircraft.

plumb line: a piece of string with a weight attached to one end of it. It is used to measure depth and to check whether something is upright. A plumb line will always hang vertically if it is allowed to hang freely.

position: the place where something or someone is.

projection: the way that map-makers show the curved surface of the earth on the flat surface of a map.

pyramid: a large stone building that has four sloping sides which meet at a point. Pyramids were used in ancient Egypt as burial places for kings and queens.

radar: a way of finding the position of an object when radio waves are sent out. They meet an object and bounce back to the radar set.

radar-controlled: given instructions by people using radar.

rectangle: a flat shape with four staight sides at right angles to each other. The opposite sides are the same length.

relief: showing the height and depths of places on a map.

represent: to show or to stand for.

right angle: an angle of 90 degrees. The corners of a square or rectangle are right angles. If you stand upright, you are standing at right angles to the floor.

rotate: to turn around a fixed point. A bicycle wheel rotates around the hub.

satellite: an object that people have launched into space. It can send back signals to the earth.

scale: the way that the units of measurement on a map compare with the size of the land it stands for.

scanner: a spinning object, often shaped like a dish, which sends out and receives radio waves.

sea level: the height that the sea reaches halfway between low tide and high tide.

series: a set of similar things or events which happen one after another.

sextant: a measuring instrument used to set the course of a ship.

shadow: the dark shape thrown on something when an object comes between it and the source of light.

sonar: a way of finding the position of an object underwater. When sound waves are sent out, they meet an object and bounce back to the sonar set.

sphere: a round object that is shaped like a ball. The earth is a sphere.

surface: the top or outside of something.

surveyor: a person who measures land and buildings in order to make maps or plans.

tax, -es: money or goods that have to be given to others in order to pay for services.

telescope: an instrument which you look through to make distant objects, such as the moon or the stars, appear bigger. Never point a telescope at the sun — you will damage your eyes.

tomb: a grave, a place where a body is buried.

transponder: a radio instrument which receives a special signal and sends back a reply.

vellum: a material made from the skins of young animals such as calves.

wheelhouse: the part of a ship from which it is steered.

Index